Understanding Artificial Intelligence (AI) For Curious Kids

Alireza Saffarzadeh

Published by Alireza Saffarzadeh, 2024.

While every precaution has been taken in the preparation of this book, the publisher assumes no responsibility for errors or omissions, or for damages resulting from the use of the information contained herein.

UNDERSTANDING ARTIFICIAL INTELLIGENCE (AI) FOR CURIOUS KIDS

First edition. December 15, 2024.

Copyright © 2024 Alireza Saffarzadeh.

Written by Alireza Saffarzadeh.

Table of Contents

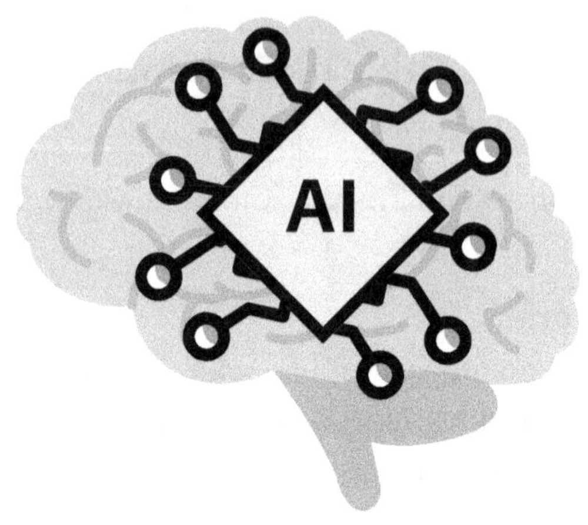

Introduction To AI

This book is about a special idea called **Artificial Intelligence**, or **AI** for short. We will begin by introducing the history of AI and how people have always been excited about creating smart tools and objects to make life easier, safer, and more comfortable. We will then explain how AI works and how it makes decisions. You will also discover that AI can do complicated tasks in many different ways to make our daily lives easier and more fun.

We will look at how AI is used in medicine, cars, games, sensing, safety, education, the arts, space, and the environment. Then, you will get to answer some fun questions and do activities that help you connect what you have learned to your everyday life.

Before we talk more about AI, let's talk about the word "**artificial**" in **Artificial Intelligence.** The word "artificial" means something made by people, not nature. For example, think about a toy car. It does not grow on trees or come from the ground. It is made in a factory by people, which makes it artificial. In contrast, things like apples, dogs, or crows are not artificial. They are made by nature. Therefore, they are real.

These are real.

What does "intelligence" mean?

Intelligence is the ability to think, learn, and solve problems. You use your intelligence every day when you figure out how to build something with blocks, learn new words, answer a math question, or decide what to do next in a game.

Now, what is Artificial Intelligence?

Artificial Intelligence, or AI, means making smart robots that can think and learn, just like we do. A robot is a type of machine that can move and do tasks, sometimes looking like a person or a toy. These smart robots can look at information, make choices, and even get better at new things—almost like how our brains learn and improve. However, AI is not the same as the real brain you have.

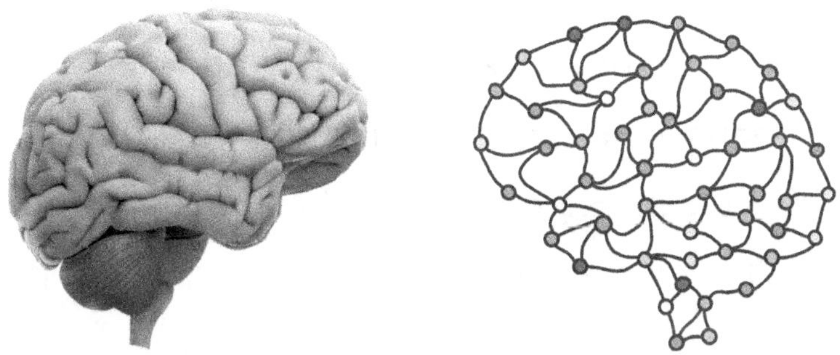

Human Brain versus **Artificial Intelligence**

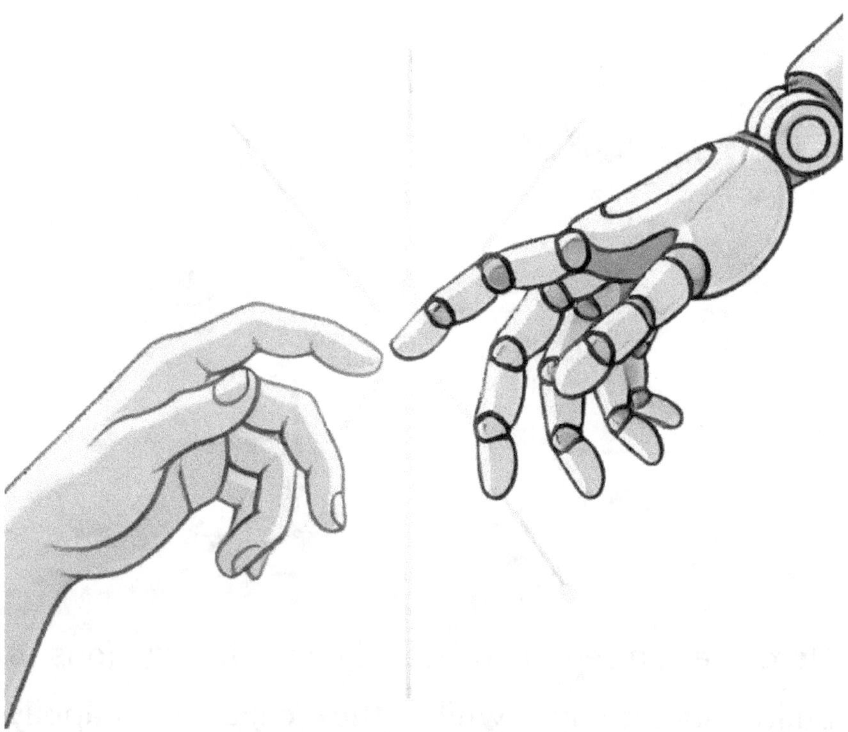

AI can learn skills, make decisions, and help us, but it doesn't feel emotions like happiness, sadness, or excitement the way humans do. It just follows the rules and data it was given.

Even though AI is very smart, it can't come up with new ideas on its own. It can help us build things or create designs, but it can't invent brand-new things like humans can. That's what makes humans so special. We can use our creativity to imagine things that don't even exist yet.

Here, we can see the robot following instructions to build something, while the child is happily imagining new and creative ideas.

But robots and machines were not always so smart. In ancient stories, there were magical creations that could move, talk, and act just like real living creatures. These stories showed how people have always been excited about creating machines that seem alive. Even though they didn't have the tools we have today, their big imaginations helped start the ideas that led to the robots and smart machines we know today.

For example, Greek mythology includes tales of Talos, a giant automaton made of bronze, who was created to protect the island of Crete from pirates and invaders.

In China, a very clever man named Yan Shi built a life-sized, human-shaped figure and showed it to the king. This mechanical person could move its arms and legs, blink its eyes, and even sing.

These old stories show that people have always been excited about the idea of robots and smart machines. Even though they didn't have the technology we have today, they imagined all sorts of wonderful machines that could move and act like real living beings. These early ideas are the foundation of the amazing world of Artificial Intelligence we know today, where machines can actually think, learn, and do amazing things.

The modern history of AI began in the mid-20th century. In 1956, John McCarthy, an American computer and cognitive scientist, organized a conference at Dartmouth College in the U.S., where the term "Artificial Intelligence" was first used.

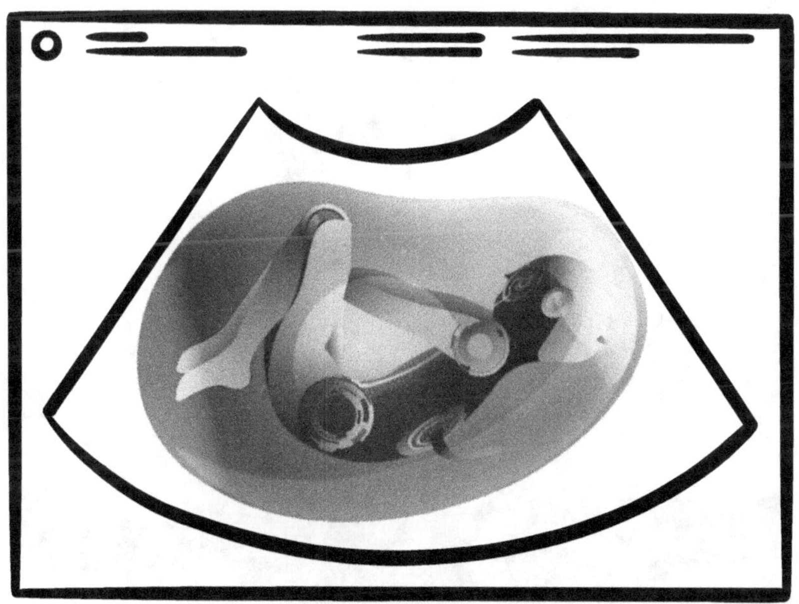

This event marked the birth of AI as a field of study, and those who attended became leaders in AI research for many years.

At first, AI scientists tried to make computers solve problems by giving them lots of rules, like a big set of instructions. But in the 1980s, scientists figured out how to help computers learn from information. This is called "machine learning."

Then, in the 2010s, they made another big jump with "deep learning." This is where computers use something called "neural networks" to think, which works a little more like the cells in a human brain.

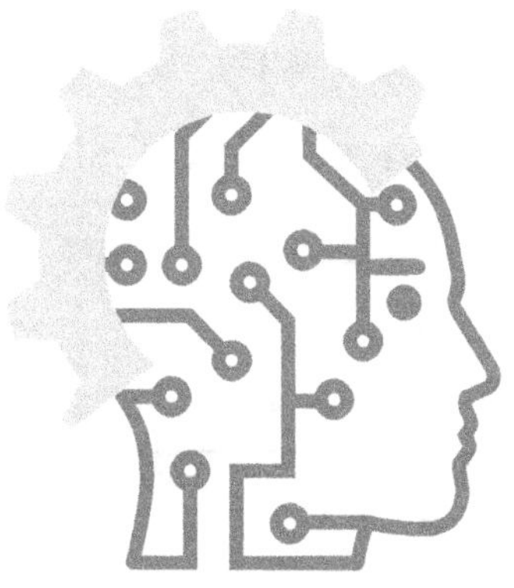

How AI works

As mentioned before, AI means making computer systems capable of doing complex tasks that usually only humans can do, like thinking, making choices, or solving problems. Let's see how it works.

First, think about how you learn new things. You learn by watching, listening, and practicing, right?

AI learns in a similar way by looking at lots of examples. For instance, if you show an AI lots of pictures of cats and dogs, it can learn to tell the difference between them.

Learning from Examples

Imagine you want to teach a robot how to draw different shapes, like circles and squares. First, you show the robot lots of pictures: big circles, small circles, black squares, blue squares, and more.

The robot looks at all these pictures carefully and starts to notice patterns. It sees that circles are round with no corners, while squares have four equal sides and four corners.

After looking at lots of pictures, the robot tries to draw a circle and a square by itself. Sometimes, it might make mistakes, like drawing an oval instead of a circle or a rectangle instead of a square. You help the robot by showing it more pictures (called input or data) and correcting its mistakes. The robot learns from these corrections and gets better at drawing the shapes.

Eventually, the robot becomes really good at drawing perfect circles and squares because it has learned from all the examples you showed it. Just like how you learn to draw by practicing and looking at pictures, AI learns by looking at many examples and practicing until it gets things right.

Understanding Words and Pictures

AI can understand words and pictures, just like we do. Let's look at some examples:

When you talk to a voice assistant like Siri or Alexa, you might say, "Play my favorite song." AI listens to your words, understands what you want, and starts playing your favorite song.

Imagine you have a bunch of pictures, and you show one of them to AI. If you show a picture of a tree, AI knows it's a tree. How? Because it has seen many pictures of trees before and remembers them.

AI can also understand sentences. If you say, "What's the weather today?" AI knows you want to know if it's sunny or rainy. It checks the weather and tells you, "It's sunny today!"

If you ask AI, "How do you spell 'elephant'?" it listens to your question and tells you the correct spelling. It's like having an assistant.

Imagine you have a drawing app on your tablet. You draw a picture of a dog, and then you ask AI, "What did I draw?" The AI looks closely at your drawing and thinks about all the pictures of dogs it has seen before. It compares your drawing with what it knows, and then says, "You drew a dog!" But sometimes, if your drawing looks a little different, AI might not be sure. You can help by giving it more examples, so it gets better at recognizing different dogs, no matter how they're drawn. The more examples AI sees, the smarter it gets at knowing what you've drawn.

In all cases, AI uses its memory of many examples to understand what we say and recognize what we show it. It's like having a smart assistant who can talk and look at pictures with you!

AI keeps getting smarter the more it sees and hears, making it a super helpful friend for finding answers, learning new things, and even playing games with you!

Making Decisions

AI can make decisions by thinking about different choices, just like we do. For example, imagine you have a smart machine named Robo who helps you pick what to wear each day. When you wake up, Robo checks the weather forecast. If it's sunny and warm, Robo suggests wearing a t-shirt and shorts. If it's rainy and cold, Robo tells you to wear a raincoat and boots.

Robo makes these smart decisions by looking at the weather information and thinking about what would be the best clothes to wear. Just like you use your brain to decide, AI uses information to make helpful choices.

Imagine you have a robot assistant named Bot who helps plan your day. Every day, Bot looks at your schedule and suggests activities. If you have lots of schoolwork, Bot might suggest starting with the hardest tasks. If you have free time, Bot might recommend having playtime outside or reading. Just like we use our brains to make decisions, AI uses information to help you make smart choices.

Improving Over Time

Imagine you have a robot that helps you bake cookies. The first time, it might not mix the dough just right or forget to set the oven temperature. But each time you bake together, the robot remembers how you like the cookies to turn out—soft in the middle and crispy on the edges! Over time, the robot learns from you and improves, helping you make the perfect batch of cookies every time. Just like you learn from practice and examples, AI learns from 'data' to get better each time.

The more data it looks at, the better it gets at understanding and making good guesses. This is why having lots of information (data) is so important for helping AI learn and get better.

As a second example, imagine a toy box filled with all kinds of toys. Each toy represents a piece of data. Inside the box, there are cars, dolls, and blocks. A child and a smart robot want to sort the toys into groups: cars, dolls, and blocks.

The child feels confident and excited about sorting the toys, while the robot looks curious and eager to learn from the child. Together, they make a great team!

The child and the robot begin the task of sorting them into different categories. The robot, eager to help, starts placing the toys into groups.

With a smile, the robot starts grouping the toys. But as they sort, the robot makes a mistake at first, placing a car next to a soft doll. The child gently says, "No, that goes over there with the cars!" The robot looks a little confused but is eager to learn from the child's guidance.

Together, they go through each toy, and the robot starts to understand where each toy belongs.

But over time, the robot learns from its mistakes and begins sorting the toys correctly. The robot is now able to place each toy in the right category, just as AI improves by learning from data.

Just like in school where you learn new things every day and get better at reading, writing, or math, AI learns from its experiences. It keeps practicing and improving, which helps it become really good at understanding and solving problems.

As mentioned before, the process of learning and getting better is called Machine Learning. This is why AI can do so many amazing things, like helping doctors, driving cars, and even playing games with us!

How does AI use data to make decisions?

In AI, something called an **algorithm** tells AI what to do with the data or information it gets. An algorithm is like step-by-step instructions for learning and making decisions. It shows AI how to use the data to solve problems or make smart choices. The algorithm is in the middle of everything! Without it, AI wouldn't know what to do with all the information it receives. The more AI uses these algorithms, the better it gets at solving problems quickly and accurately.

For example, let's look at this simple algorithm for finding the biggest number between two choices:

1. **Start**

2. **Look at two numbers:** Let's call them **A** and **B**.

3. **Compare the numbers:**

- If **A** is bigger than **B**, say, "A is bigger!"

- If **B** is bigger than **A**, say, "B is bigger!"

4. **End**

Below, we show the same algorithm as a flowchart.

Flowchart of Finding the Biggest Number

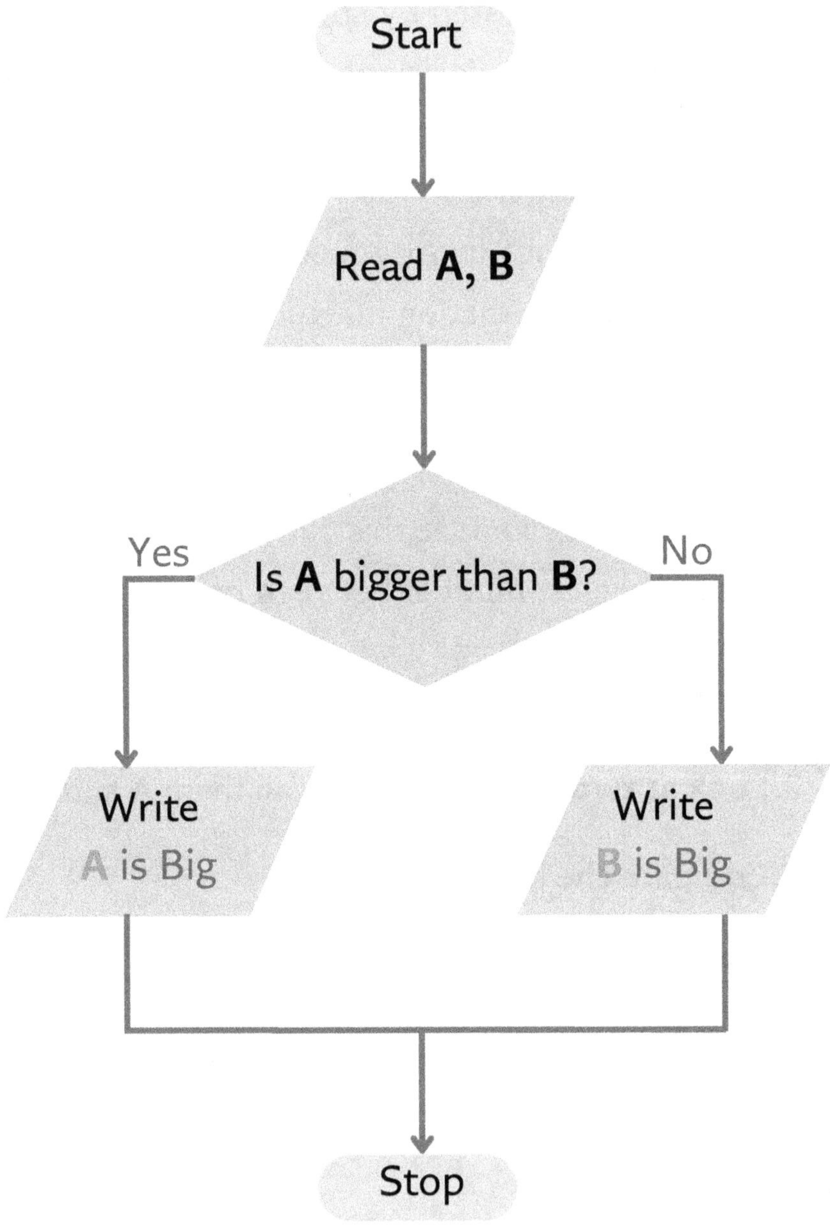

Now, think of algorithms as a recipe for making pita bread. Just like a recipe has steps to follow so you can make tasty bread, an algorithm has steps to solve a problem. The ingredients are like the data or inputs, and the final pita bread is the result or output.

By following the recipe (algorithm) correctly, you can achieve the desired outcome, whether it's delicious pita bread or solving a problem using AI.

Here is the step-by-step **Algorithm (recipe) for Making Pita Bread:**

1. **Start**
2. **Gather Ingredients:**
    - 500g flour
    - 7g yeast
    - 200ml water
    - 20ml olive oil
    - 1/2 teaspoon salt
3. **Mix Ingredients:**
    - Combine flour, yeast, water, olive oil, and salt in a bowl.
4. **Knead Dough:**
    - Knead the mixture until it forms a smooth dough.
5. **Let Dough Rest:**
    - Cover the dough and let it rest for 20 minutes.
6. **Cut Dough:**
    - Cut the dough into 10 pieces.
7. **Roll Dough:**
    - Roll each piece into a circle.
8. **Bake:**
    - Bake the circles in a preheated oven on high for 7 minutes.
9. **End with Pita Bread**

Step-by-Step Guide:
Pita Bread Algorithm (recipe) in Pictures

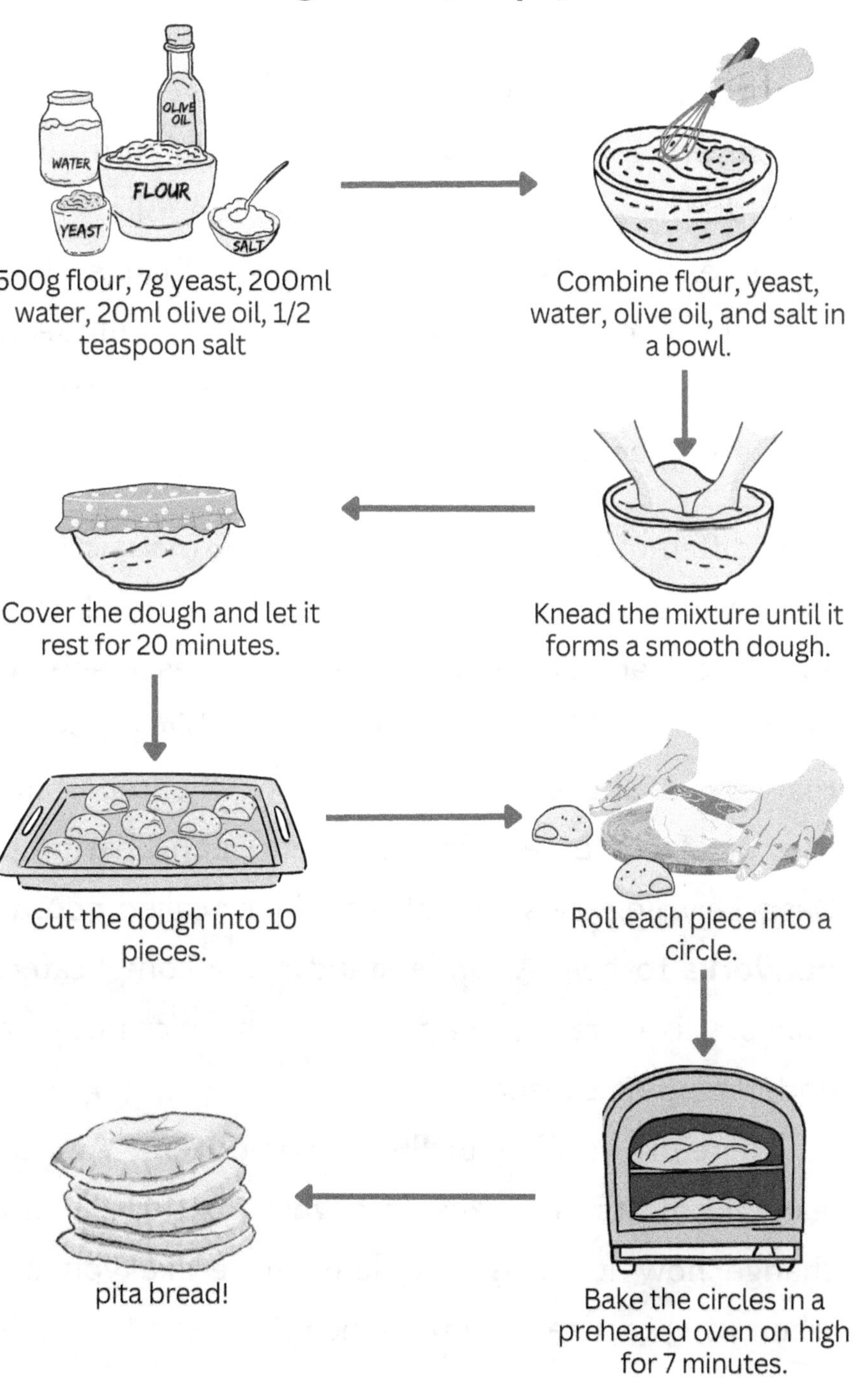

500g flour, 7g yeast, 200ml water, 20ml olive oil, 1/2 teaspoon salt

Combine flour, yeast, water, olive oil, and salt in a bowl.

Cover the dough and let it rest for 20 minutes.

Knead the mixture until it forms a smooth dough.

Cut the dough into 10 pieces.

Roll each piece into a circle.

pita bread!

Bake the circles in a preheated oven on high for 7 minutes.

The Difference Between Computers and AI

You might wonder, if both computers and AI use algorithms, what makes them different? Well, **computers** follow **fixed instructions** (algorithms). They do the same thing every time, like following a recipe exactly. They don't learn or change. For example, if you tell a computer to add two numbers, it will always follow the same steps without learning and getting better.

AI is different because it uses **learning instructions** (algorithms) that help it get better over time! This ability to learn and improve is known as **Machine Learning**. Machine Learning is like a big umbrella that covers all the ways AI can learn. One important part of Machine Learning is called **Deep Learning**. Deep Learning uses special techniques called **neural networks** to help AI understand really complicated things, like recognizing faces in pictures or understanding speech.

Therefore, **unlike ordinary computers, AI** can learn from its mistakes, recognize patterns, and change how it solves problems—just like you do when you practice something new.

Let's talk about something fun—**cats** and **dogs**!

In the picture below, do you see a cat or a dog?

How do you know if it's a cat or a dog?

You've probably seen lots of them, so you've learned how to tell them apart.

We want to teach computers to do the same thing!

Just like you, computers need to see lots of pictures to learn how to recognize cats and dogs.

But even people sometimes get mixed up, and computers can make mistakes too!

To help the computer learn, we show it the important parts of a picture, like the shape of the ears or the size of the nose.

The computer remembers those details to figure out if a new picture is of a cat, dog, or something else. This is called **object recognition**, and it helps computers understand what they see!

Below is the relationship between artificial intelligence, machine learning, deep learning, and artificial neural networks.

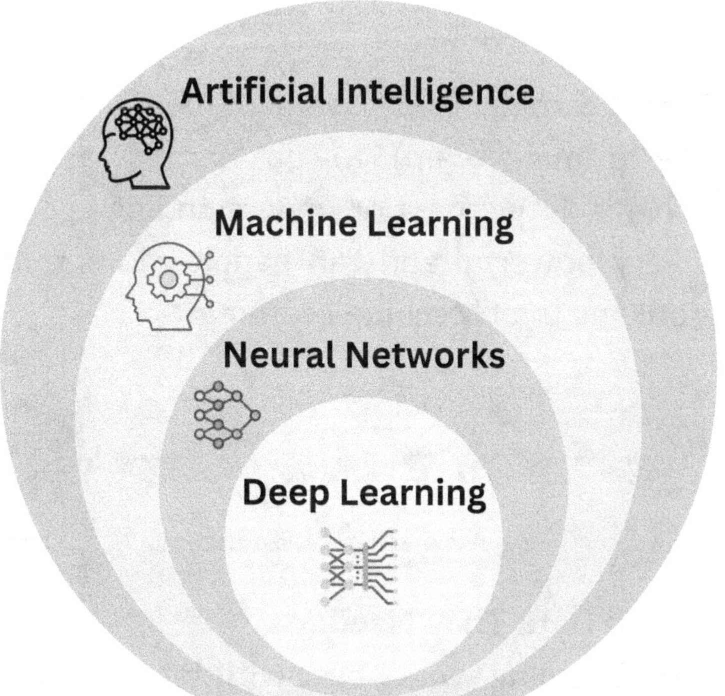

Now, let's discuss the **key differences** between **Machine Learning** and **Deep Learning**.

What They Do:
- Machine Learning uses special math (algorithms) to find patterns in data and make guesses or decisions based on new data. It can be used with help from people (supervised) or without help (unsupervised).

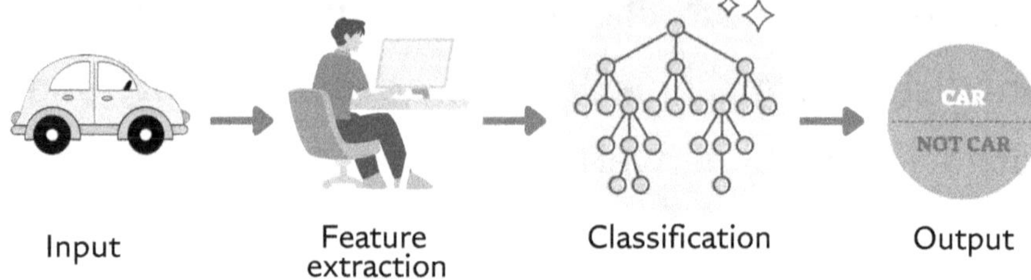

- Deep Learning uses layers of neural networks (like a mini brain) to do harder tasks, like recognizing pictures or understanding speech. It is very powerful and can handle more complex problems than Machine Learning.

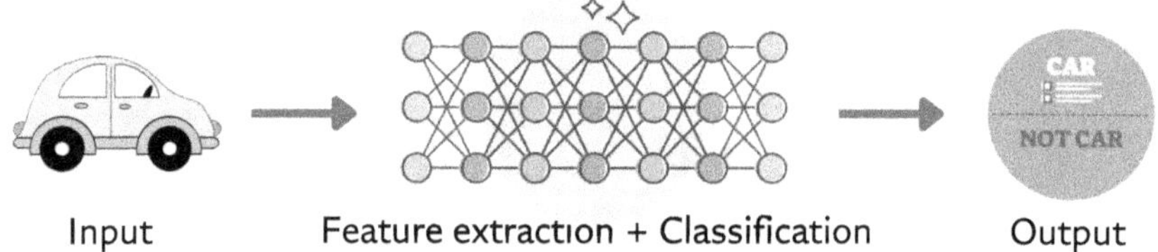

How Much Data They Need:

- Deep Learning works best with lots of data (like millions of pictures), while Machine Learning can work with smaller sets of data. Using deep learning with small data can lead to bad results, so Machine Learning is better for smaller tasks.

Complexity:

- Deep Learning is more complex and can solve bigger problems like understanding voice commands or making recommendations. Machine Learning is simpler and handles smaller tasks.

Hardware Requirements:

- Deep Learning needs very powerful computers with special parts called Graphics Processing Units (GPUs) to work. Machine Learning can use regular computers, which makes it less expensive. So, when deciding between Machine Learning and Deep Learning, you should ask, "Do I have a strong computer and a lot of labeled data?". If you don't have either of these, it's better to use Machine Learning because Deep Learning is more complicated. For example, you will need at least a few thousand pictures to get good results with Deep Learning, and a strong computer (with a GPU) to help it work faster.

Deep Learning Requirements

Time to Learn:

- **Deep Learning** takes much longer to learn (hours or even weeks), while **Machine Learning** can learn faster, sometimes in seconds or minutes. This also makes Deep Learning more expensive to run.

100%

Progress of Learning Time
in **Machine Learning**

10%

Progress of Learning Time
in **Deep Learning**

Choosing Important Information :

- In **Machine Learning**, scientists need to choose which parts of the data are important to help the computer learn better. This is called **feature engineering**.

- In **Deep Learning**, the computer figures out which information is important all by itself, so no extra work is needed.

Different Uses:

- **Machine Learning** works well with data that's in tables, like numbers or lists.

- **Deep Learning** is better for things like pictures, speech, or text. AI scientists are developing a device for people with visual impairment that uses deep learning and computer vision to describe the world around them.

Summary:

In this chapter, we discussed how AI can learn from examples and understand things like words and pictures, similar to how we learn new things by practicing. AI takes information (or data), follows instructions (the algorithm), and improves over time by learning from mistakes. This process is called machine learning, where AI gets better at identifying objects, such as telling the difference between a cat and a dog.

We also talked about deep learning, a special kind of machine learning that helps AI understand more complex things, like recognizing faces or voices.

In the next chapter, we'll discover how AI affects our everyday lives, from helping us at home to improving the technology we use every day!

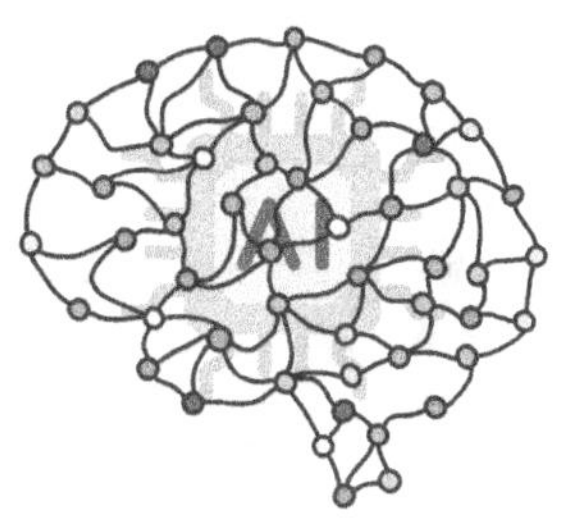

AI in Everyday Life

AI in Medicine

AI helps doctors take better care of people by looking at a lot of medical information, finding patterns, and suggesting the best ways to treat someone. Imagine a doctor trying to figure out why someone is sick. AI can help by looking at things like test results, medical records, or even pictures like X-rays. It can spot problems, like a broken bone or a sickness, that might be hard for doctors to see right away.

For example, when someone hurts their arm, AI can look at an X-ray and quickly show where the bone is broken.

AI helps doctors know what's wrong faster, so they can start fixing the problem and help the person feel better sooner.

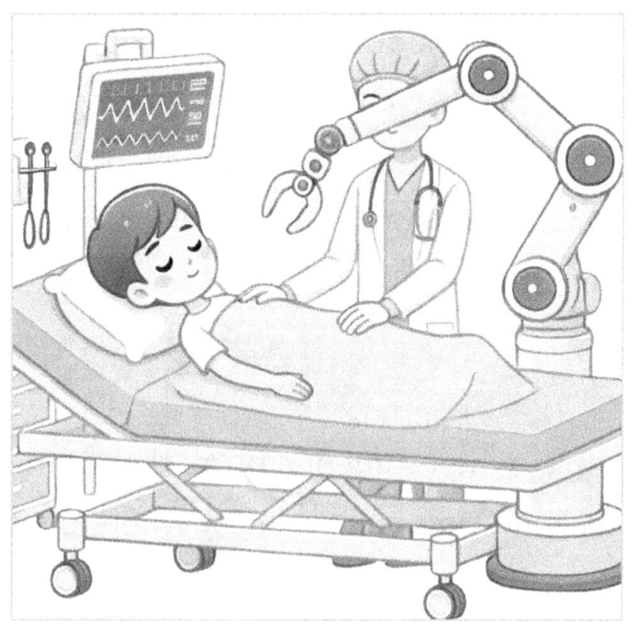

AI in Self-Driving Cars

AI helps cars drive by themselves. Self-driving cars have special eyes, like cameras and sensors, that help them see what's around them. These eyes can see other cars, people, traffic signs, and what the road looks like.

- The AI in the car acts like a brain. It "thinks" about what the car's "eyes" (like cameras and sensors) see.

- It can tell if there are other cars around, how fast they're moving, and whether the car should stop or keep going.

- The car's brain then makes decisions, like when to stop, go, or turn, so it stays safe on the road.

The more the AI drives, the smarter it gets. It learns from all the trips it takes, so it can drive better and safer each time, all by themselves.

AI in Games

AI helps the computer play games with you. When you play a game on your tablet, computer, or video game console, there's often an AI working behind the scenes to play the game with you.

Imagine teaching a friend how to play a game. At first, they might not be very good, but the more they play, the better they get. AI works the same way. This helps the AI get smarter and come up with better ways to play against you.

When you're playing, you make decisions about what to do next, like where to move your character or which card to play. AI does this too. For example, in a game of chess, the AI thinks about all the different moves it could make and picks the one that has the best chance of winning.

Sometimes, AI isn't just someone you play against; it's your teammate. In some games, you and the AI work together to win, like passing a level or solving a puzzle. The AI can help you figure out what to do or give you extra help when things get hard.

Question: What games do you play where AI helps you?

AI in Sensing

AI can 'see' and 'hear' like we do, but it uses special tools to help. AI uses cameras to see, just like our eyes help us see. So, when you smile at a camera, AI can see your happy face and know you're smiling. It can even tell if you look sad or surprised.

AI also uses microphones to hear, just like our ears help us listen. When you talk to it, AI listens carefully. For example, if you ask a question, AI hears your voice and then tries its best to give you a good answer, like when you ask a smart speaker, 'What's the weather?'

AI and Safety

AI also helps keep us safe in many ways. For example, some homes have special cameras that watch what's happening outside or inside the house.

AI helps these cameras see if someone is there who shouldn't be, like a stranger, and it can tell us if something looks wrong. This helps keep our homes safe when we are away or sleeping.

When we use the internet, like playing games or watching videos, AI can help protect our personal information, like your name, your age, or where you live. AI can recognize when someone suspicious tries to access your information, like hackers or people who shouldn't have it.

If AI notices something strange, it can block them from getting in. This way, only the right people can see the information, and it helps us stay safe.

AI in Education

AI helps students learn new things in a fun and easy way. Imagine you're using a learning app on your tablet to practice math or reading. The app might notice that you are really good at adding numbers but need a little more practice with reading. The AI in the app is super smart and helps you by suggesting new things to learn or practice. It might show you a new book to read or give you more fun math problems to solve.

The more you use the app, the better the AI gets at knowing what you already know and what you need to practice. It's like having your very own teacher inside the app, helping you get better and better each time you play and learn.

AI in Robots

AI helps robots work in many different ways. In some homes, robots can help with cleaning. Imagine a small robot moving around the house, sweeping the floor or vacuuming up dirt, just like a tiny helper. These robots use AI to know where to go and what to clean. They can even move around furniture and go back to their charging station when they're done. It's like having a little robot friend that keeps your house tidy.

In factories, robots can do tough jobs that might be too hard or dangerous for people. For example, a robot might lift heavy things or work in places where it's too hot or too high for humans to go. AI helps these robots know what to do and how to stay safe while working.

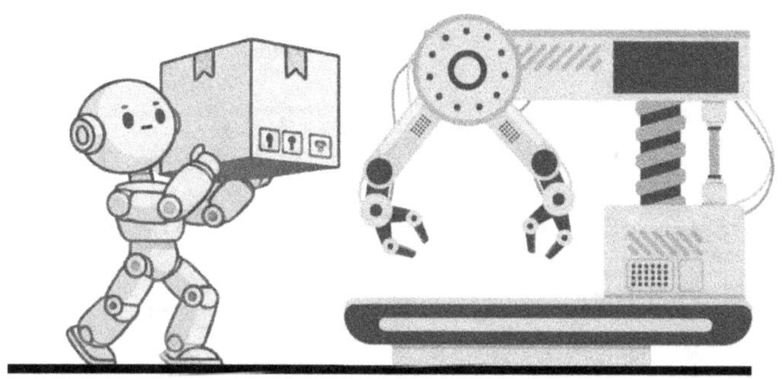

AI and Arts

AI helps create fun things, like music, drawings, and even stories. For example, AI can help a musician create a new song. It listens to lots of music, then helps the musician put sounds together to make a beautiful tune.

AI can also help painters create cool pictures. It looks at many different kinds of art and then helps artists mix colors and shapes to make new and exciting paintings.

AI can even help tell stories. Imagine sitting down to write a fun story, and AI helps you come up with great ideas for characters and adventures.

Therefore, AI not only makes hard things simple but also helps artists and musicians be super creative, making fun and amazing things to see and hear.

AI in Space

Imagine astronauts flying to faraway planets or moons. It can be hard for them to explore alone, so AI steps in to help.

AI controls **rovers** - special robots that move around on planets like Mars. The rover looks at rocks, dirt, and the land to learn what the planet is made of.

AI helps the rover decide where to go and what to explore. Even when astronauts are far away, AI works fast to check the information the rover sends back. It helps find exciting things like clues about water or signs of life on distant planets.

AI in the Environment

AI is not just helping people, but it's also helping our planet. Here are some ways AI is being used to take care of the environment:

- In a forest with elephants, tigers, and birds, AI helps scientists watch over the animals. Using cameras and special tools, AI can spot animals and even know which kind they are. This keeps the animals safe and makes sure they have enough space to live.

- In our homes, AI can help us save energy, which is good for the environment. AI can learn when we usually turn on the lights or use the air conditioner, and it can help us use just the right amount of energy. This way, we don't waste energy, and it helps keep our planet healthy.

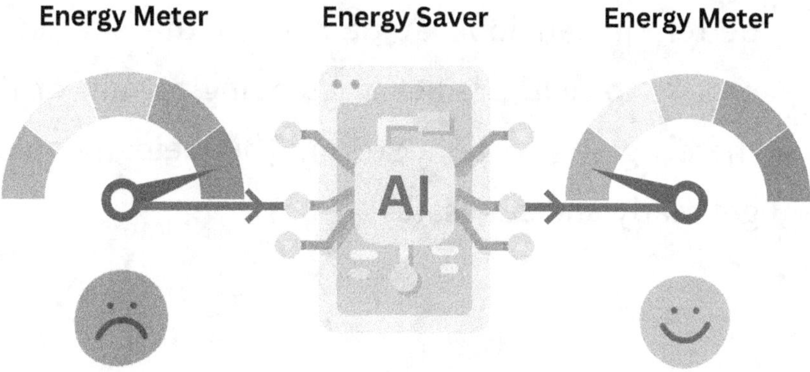

- AI can also help plant trees! Special AI-powered drones can fly over big areas of land and plant seeds in the ground. This is a super-fast way to grow forests and make the world greener.

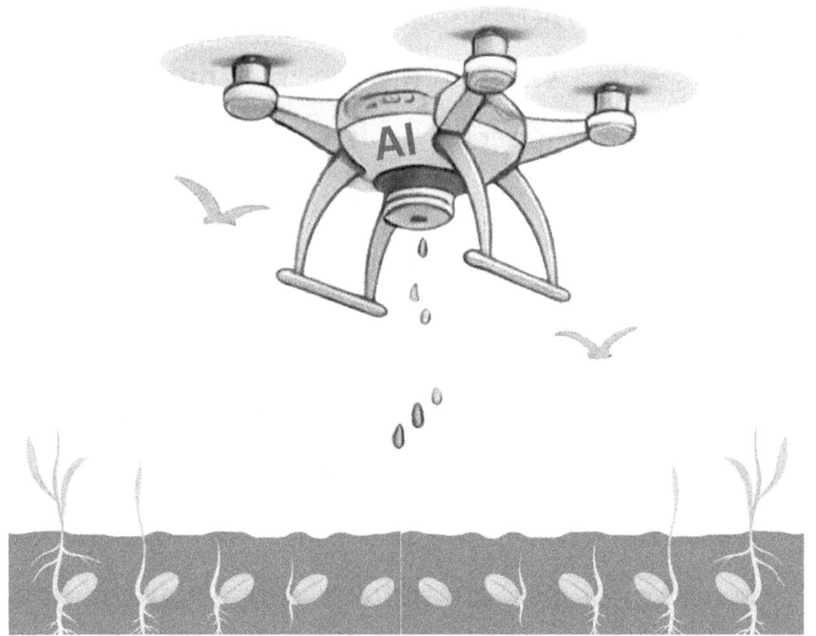

- AI helps scientists understand the weather better. It can look at data from the sky and oceans to help predict if it's going to rain or if there's going to be a storm. This helps people get ready and stay safe.

- AI can help clean up our planet by finding places that are dirty or polluted. For example, AI can look at pictures of the ocean and find spots where there is too much plastic or trash. Then, people can go and clean it up, making the earth a better place for everyone.

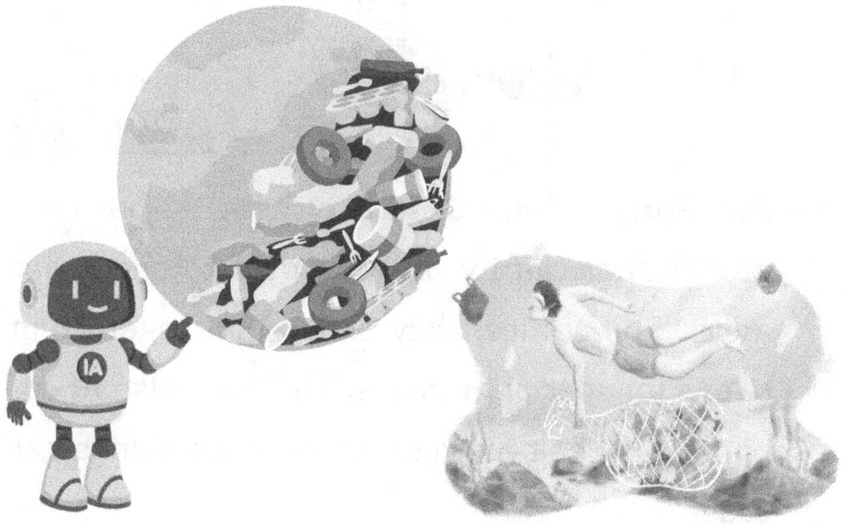

AI in the Military

AI isn't just for games, space, or medicine—it's also making a big difference in the military. It helps different teams like the Army, Navy, Air Force, and even space and cyber teams do their jobs better and keep people safer.

- **Army**: AI helps soldiers by using robot vehicles that can travel on the ground by themselves to gather information, carry supplies, and even help in battles.

- **Air Force**: The Air Force uses AI-powered drones that can fly on their own to check out areas. Sometimes, they even work together in teams for special missions. There are also AI co-pilots that help human pilots when things get tough.

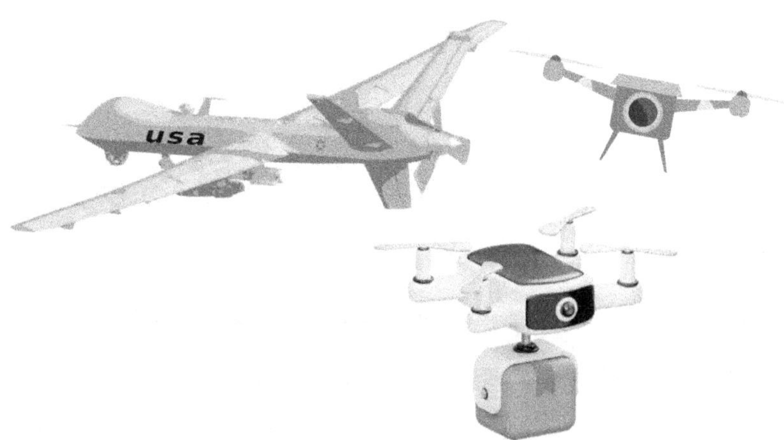

- **Navy**: The Navy uses AI for self-operating ships and submarines that can patrol the seas and help spot enemy submarines. AI also helps make sure ships have enough supplies, even when they're far from land.

So, AI is also a big help in keeping people safe by supporting soldiers, ships, planes, and even satellites in space!

The Limitations of AI

AI can do amazing things, but it has some downsides, too. For example, AI doesn't have feelings or common sense like people do. This means it can sometimes make mistakes or misunderstand things that seem obvious to us. Also, because AI learns from the information it's given, if it learns from wrong information, it could make decisions that aren't fair or correct.

Since AI can do certain jobs, some people worry it might even take away jobs in the future.

Another downside is that people may rely on AI too much and forget to double-check its work.

Finally, some people are concerned that if we use AI too much, it could start to make too many choices for us, taking away some of our control. People want to make sure we stay in charge of important decisions and use AI as a tool to help us, not to control us.

Staying Safe with AI Online

AI can be really helpful, like when you ask a voice assistant to play your favorite song or when an app suggests fun games to try. But just like when you cross the street, you need to be careful and stay safe when using AI online. Here are some tips to help you:

- Before using any new app or talking to a voice assistant, always ask an adult if it's okay. They can help make sure it's safe and fun for you to use.

- If an app or voice assistant asks you for personal information like your name, address, or school, don't share it. Always check with a grown-up before giving out any details about yourself.

- When you use voice assistants, remember to be kind and polite, just like when you talk to people. Even though AI isn't a person, it's good to practice being friendly.

- Some apps and games are designed especially for kids, and they're super safe to use. Stick to these apps, and avoid downloading anything without checking with an adult first.

- When you're finished using an app or voice assistant, make sure to turn it off. This helps keep your device safe and saves battery too.

The Future of AI

Imagine a world where AI can do even more amazing things! Today, AI helps us with things like driving cars, finding information, and even exploring space. But in the future, AI might help us solve even bigger problems and make life easier in ways we haven't thought of yet.

What if AI could help invent new ways to protect animals and nature? Or create new ways for kids to learn that feel just like playing games? Maybe AI will even help us discover things deep under the ocean or far away in space, or create robots that can help us at home with chores or make us laugh when we feel sad.

The cool thing about AI is that it keeps getting smarter. People are always thinking of new ways to make AI more helpful and creative. And one day, you might be the one inventing something new for AI to do!

Imagine and Dream: *What would you like AI to help with? Maybe it's a robot that can read stories to you, or an AI that helps you take care of pets. The future of **AI is all about ideas**, and **your ideas could change the world.***

Fun Questions and Activities

Question: What do doctors use AI for?

Activity: Draw a picture of a robot helping a doctor.

Question: How can AI help doctors?

Activity: Pretend you're a doctor using AI to find out what's making someone sick. Draw what you would do.

Question: How can AI be your friend when playing a game?

Activity: Imagine you're playing a game with a robot friend. What kind of game would you play with a robot friend? Draw or describe it.

Question: How does AI help cars drive by themselves?

Activity: Draw a picture of a car driving by itself. Where is it going?

Question: What can AI do in your house to help?

Activity: Draw a picture of a robot cleaning your room. What is the robot's name?

Question: What does AI help astronauts do?

Activity: Pretend you are an astronaut with a robot helper. What would you discover on another planet?

Question: How does AI help you learn new things?

Activity: Create a fun quiz with questions about your favorite subject. Ask a friend or family member to try it.

Question: What can AI help you learn better in school?

Activity: Draw or write about something new you learned with the help of AI.

Question: How can AI help the Earth stay clean?

Activity: Draw a picture of a robot planting trees or cleaning a park.

Question: What should you remember to do when using AI online?

Activity: Draw a picture of yourself being safe online. What are you doing?

Question: How can AI help us save energy?

Activity: Think of one way you use energy at home. Draw how AI could help you use less energy.